Frank's Gift for the King

by **Maryann Dobeck**

illustrations by **Sam Day**

Harcourt Brace & Company

Orlando Atlanta Austin Boston San Francisco Chicago Dallas New York Toronto London

"I need a gift for the king,"
said Frank. "Something big.
Something fat. Something pink."

"No!" said Hank.
Hank was Frank's big, fat,
pink pig.

"I stink!" said Hank. "The king can't get a pink pig that stinks."

Frank put Hank in the sink.
Frank plunked and dunked Hank.
Hank sank into the suds.

Frank swung Hank into his cart.
Clank! Clank! Clank!
"I'm off to see the king," said
Frank.

Mrs. Wong stopped by.
"Nice pig, Frank!" said Mrs.
Wong. "Will you sell Hank?"

Before Frank could think,
Hank sang this song.
I'm a pig that can sing.
I'm a gift for the king.

Mr. Banks stopped by.
"Great pig," said Mr. Banks.
"Can I have Hank?"

Before Frank could think,
Hank sang this song.
   I'm a pig that can sing.
   I'm too good for the king.

"What do you think?" asked
Hank.
Frank winked at Hank.
"I think we'll go home!"

"I need a gift for the king," said
Hank. "Something that sings.
Something with wings."